The Ultimate Duct Tape Book

25 Cool & Creative Projects to Get You on a Roll!

Liz Hum

This book is available in quantity at special discounts for your group or organization. For further information, contact:

Triumph Books LLC
814 North Franklin Street
Chicago, Illinois 60610
Phone: (312) 337-0747
www.triumphbooks.com

Printed in U.S.A.

ISBN: 978-1-62937-039-2

Content developed and packaged by Rockett Media, Inc.
Writer: Liz Hum
Editor: Bob Baker
Design: Liz Hum
Cover Design by Andy Hansen

Table of Contents

The Origin of Duct Tape.....04
Supply List.......................06

Chapter One:
Wrap it Up..........08
Simple first projects that get you used to working with duct tape.

Can Caddy...................10
Drink Bottles...............14
Photo Frame................16
Notebook.....................21
Tape Art.......................26
How to Make Stickers..29

Chapter Two:
On a Roll 30
Making more advanced designs and functional objects.

Key Chain....................32
Lanyard.......................35
Tulip Pens....................38
Blossoms.....................45

Tri-Petals.....................50
Rose............................55
Petal Flower.................62
Gift Bow......................66

Chapter Three:
Stuck on You......70
Enter the world of duct tape fashion and accessories.

Feather Earrings..........72
Bangle Earrings...........76
Belt..............................80
Woven Cuff.................82
Hair Bow......................87
Wallet..........................90
Tote Bag......................98
Fabric..........................105
Charms.......................106

Stuck at Prom ®................110

The Origin

Way back, around the turn of the century (meaning the early 1900's), people used a material called "duck tape" to reinforce shoes and clothing as well as building materials. Duck tape was made with strips of cotton duck cloth, otherwise known as canvas. It's pretty much the same stuff that gets stretched over a wooden frame to make a painter's canvas. The word "tape" is misleading, though. There was no adhesive or glue backing. Instead the cotton duck was sewn into garments or wrapped and adhered with oils.

Soon, tapes were made with adhesive on one side. During World War II, a new type of adhesive tape was invented to keep ammunition cases dry. It was made of duck cloth to cut easily, polyethylene (plastic) to make it waterproof, and a rubber glue to make it sticky. Originally, it was colored olive drab (army green) to match the soldier's equipment.

# of Duct Tape

It didn't take long before the soldiers were using "duck tape" to patch and fix just about anything that needed patching and fixing. From their tents, to their boots, to their guns and their tools, duck tape came in handy on and off the battlefield. When the war was over and they came home, duck tape became a household staple as well as an industry tool.

Duck tape is famous for fixing just about anything. And now duck tape is becoming famous for making just about anything! In this book, you'll learn the simplest ways to: spruce up household fixtures, make fun crafts, construct useful items, and create fashionable accessories!

Duct Tape ...or Duck Tape?

Once civilians were using the new army tape to repair just about everything in their homes, it was colored silver with powdered aluminum and marketed to tape duct work. Large rolls of the familiar silver tape were sold as "duct tape." Today, special tapes are used to seal heating and cooling ducts that can withstand temperature fluctuations, but the name stuck. Whether you call it "duct tape" or "duck tape," it means the same thing. The only difference is in the brand and style.

Supply List

A craft knife will allow precise cuts and finely-tuned detailing.

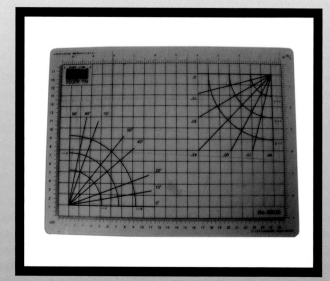

A self-healing cutting mat is used repeatedly. It will help you measure larger pieces and fabrics.

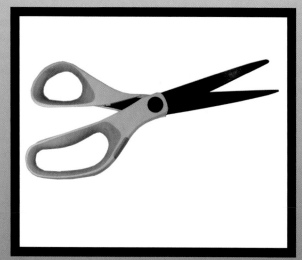

A good pair of sharp scissors will make straight, long cuts.

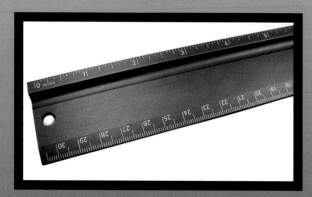

A rubber or cork-backed ruler will assist in measurements and sharp edges without slipping.

Stiff floral wire helps shape flower projects.

Common tools needed for most duct tape crafts:

A hot glue gun is useful to adhere embellishments.

Velcro strips make easy closures for bracelets and bags.

Adhesive remover is a lifesaver for cleaning all the sticky residue from your scissors and craft knife.

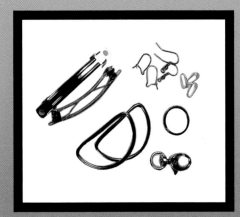

An array of barrettes, key rings, belt loops, earring hooks and pendant clasps keep fashion at your fingertips.

*Not Pictured: pens, cans, cannisters, notebooks, picture frames and painter's canvasses are used in this book to personalize and decorate.

Chapter One:
Wrap it Up

Simple first projects that get you used to working with duct tape.

Can Caddy

Materials needed: *Duct tape, scissors, cannister.*

Step one:

Take a can or cannister and remove all labels. Wash the can and let it dry thoroughly before starting.

Step two:

Flip the can on it's side and line the tape up to the top edge or lip. Press against the seam to keep the tape straight.

Step three:

Begin to roll the can away from you, as you press the tape down from the lip, outward. This should remove air bubbles.

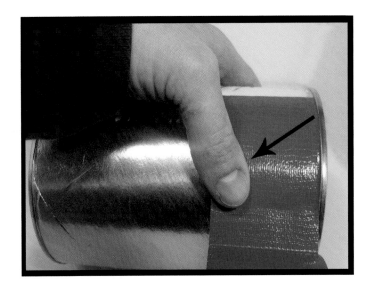

Step four:

Once you have made a complete rotation, use scissors to cut the tape.

Step five:

Repeat the process on the other side of the can, using the bottom edge as a guide. Start parallel to your first strip so that your seams will line up.

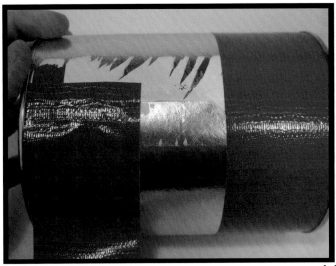

Step six:

Your can should have a strip of tape on both the top and bottom.

Step seven:

Begin to adhere your final strip of tape in the center. It should overlap the other pieces equally.

Step eight:

Make sure you keep all of the seams in the same place on the back of your can.

Step nine:

Now you have a container for your craft knife, scissors and rubber-backed ruler!

Pro Tips:

Use your craft knife and rubber-backed ruler to create thinner strips for a different look.
Add shape to the strips for flair!

Drink Bottles

Materials needed: *Duct tape, scissors, drink bottles.*

Step one:

Start by removing the labels from the water or drink bottles.

Step two:

Flip the bottle on its side and line your tape up with a rib or groove in the plastic to keep the tape level.

Step three:

Begin to roll the bottle away from you while pressing the tape down evenly.

Step four:

Once you have completed a full rotation, cut the tape with scissors or a craft knife.

Step five:

You have festive drink bottles for your next party! Guests can write their names on the tape with a permanent marker to avoid mix-ups.

Photo Frame

Materials needed: *Duct tape, frame, craft knife.*

Step one:

Remove the back and glass of a frame. Put tabs in the upright position, if needed.

Step two:

Cut a strip of tape 2 inches longer than the frame and adhere to the longest edge, making sure there is overlap on all four sides.

Step three:

Flip the frame over and cut a 90 degree angle from each outer corner, using a craft knife.

Step four:

Fold the long outer edge over and press to seal.

Step five:

Fold the shorter edge over the back and press to seal.

Step six:

Make a 90 degree cut at each inner corner with a craft knife.

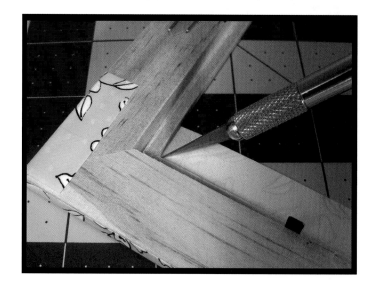

Step seven:

Fold the inner edges over and press to seal. Use your craft knife to trim any excess tape that gets in the way of the frame.

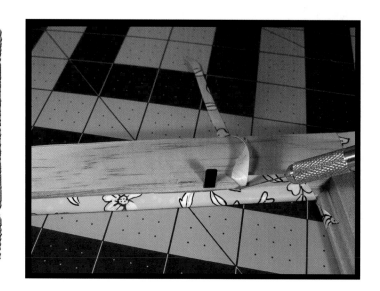

Step eight:

Repeat the process on the other long side of your frame.

Step nine:

Cut enough strips to cover the short sides of the frame and make sure they are long enough for overlap.

Step ten:

Place the strips on each side, as shown. Overlap 1/8 inch between pieces.

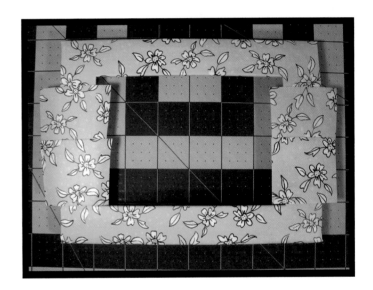

Step eleven:

Fold the pieces around the frame and press to seal. Cut any excess tape away, if needed.

Step twelve:

Put your frame back together and enjoy a unique and stylish accent!

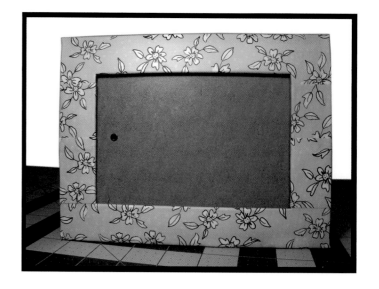

Pro Tips:

Adhere 3D elements to your frame for extra style points! Or use a flat frame and add magnets to the back to hang on the fridge.

Notebook

Materials needed: *Duct tape, notebook, scissors, velcro tabs.*

Step one:

Lay the first strip of tape across the top of a composition notebook leaving an extra 1/4 inch on the top and 1 inch on the side.

Step two:

Turn the notebook over, as you run the tape roll all the way around it. Leave 1 inch extra on the end. Cut with scissors.

Step three:

Fold the outer flaps over and press to seal.

Leave the top overlap alone for now.

Step four:

Continue laying the tape in rows, all the way down the notebook. Overlap 1/8 inch between each piece. Fold the outer flaps over as you go.

Step five:

On the last roll, make sure you leave 1/4 inch extra at the bottom, just like the top.

Step six:

Cut out the binding area on the top and bottom with your craft knife.

Step seven:

Next, cut away the flaps, on the top and the bottom, that were folded over onto each other.

Step eight:

Fold the excess top and bottom tape over the inner edge and press to seal.

Step nine:

To make the inside neat, lay strips of tape along the inside edges.

Step ten:

To make a close-tab, cut a 6 inch strip of tape and stick 1 inch of it to the outer back cover of the notebook, facing up.

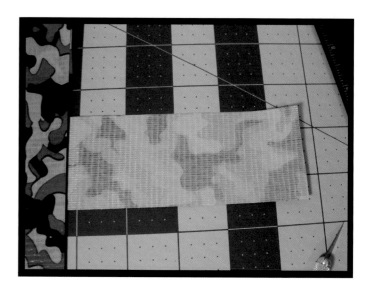

Step eleven:

Fold the piece over in half, making sure you have 1 inch adhered to the inside of the back cover.

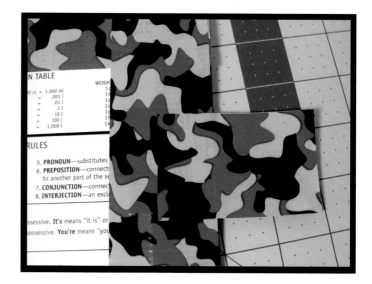

Step twelve:

Stick a piece of self-adhesive velcro on the tab, facing up. Put it's match on top of it, then close the notebook and press the tab onto the front cover.

Step thirteen:

Now you have a personalized notebook with closure.

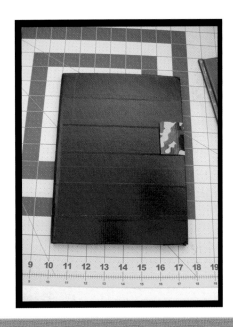

Pro Tips:

See Page 29 to make personalized stickers!

Tape Art

Materials needed: *Duct tape, canvas, craft knife.*

Step one:

Before you begin, draw a design. Lay your first strip of background tape across the top, with overlap to match the depth of the canvas.

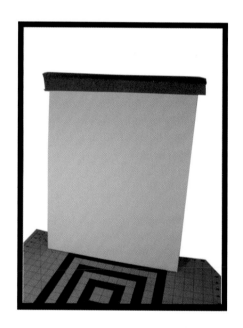

Step two:

Press both sides down over the edge, until you have a flap on the corners.

Step three:

Cut the flap off with your craft knife or scissors.

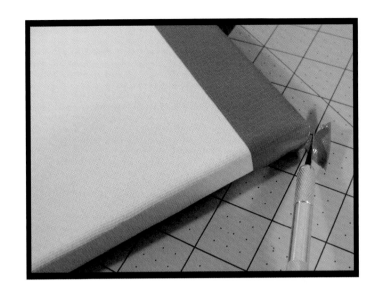

Step four:

Continue laying your background strips with 1/8 inch overlap between strips. Seal the bottom edges and corners off, the same way as the top.

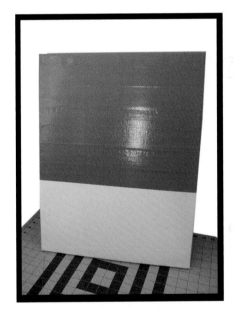

Step five:

See page 29 ("How to Make Stickers") to create the designs. Lay your stickers from the background to the foreground.

Step six:

Finish your piece and add optional embellishments or mixed media.
Start a gallery!

Pro Tips:

The options are endless, from the abstract to the ornate. Mix up media to create a collage or add 3D tape embellishments from this book!

How to Make Stickers

1.

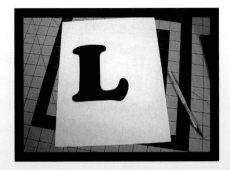

Print out a design you want to use and scale it to your desired size.

2.

Use your craft knife to carefully and precisely cut the paper backing away.

3.

You now have a stencil to work with. It can be used repetedly.

4.

Roll out your tape onto the cutting mat, sticky side down.

5.

Make a square slightly larger than your stencil and lay them one on top of the next with 1/4 inch overlap.

6.

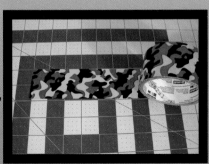

Tape your stencil on top of your tape square, using removable tape.

7.

Use your craft knife to carefully and precisely cut around the stencil.

8.

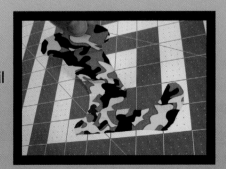

Remove the stencil and peel off your sticker!

Chapter Two: On a Roll

Making more advanced designs and functional objects.

Key Chain

Materials needed: *Duct tape, key ring.*

Step one:

Cut two 6 inch strips of tape on your cutting mat.

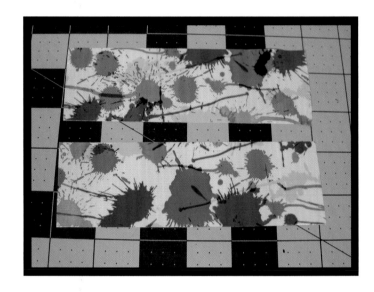

Step two:

Turn the tape over, one at a time, and fold lengthwise, halfway up.
Start in the middle and press out to the right.

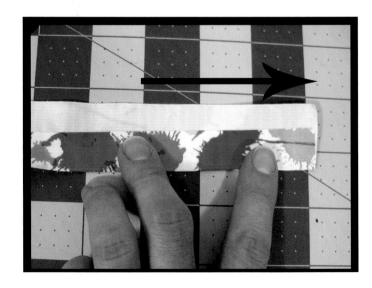

Step three:

Then, press down from the middle to the left. This should reduce creases and unevenness.

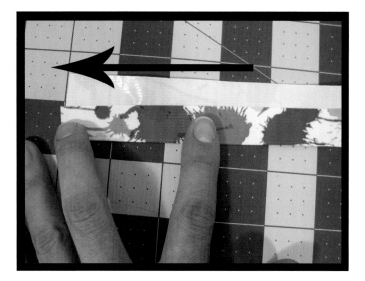

Step four:

Fold the other side of the tape over the top. Repeat steps two and three for the second strip.

Step five:

Cut a strip of tape 2 inches long on your cutting mat and slice it in half, lengthwise.

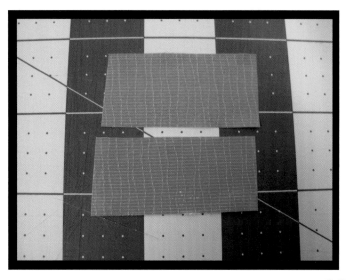

Step six:

Use one of the smaller pieces to adhere the two strips together.

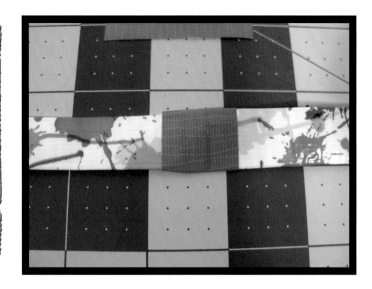

Step seven:

Fold the new, long strip in half and fish both free ends through a key ring. Fold the free edges upward over the ring.

Step eight:

Use the second small strip to adhere the edges to the loop and you have a key chain you can hang anywhere.

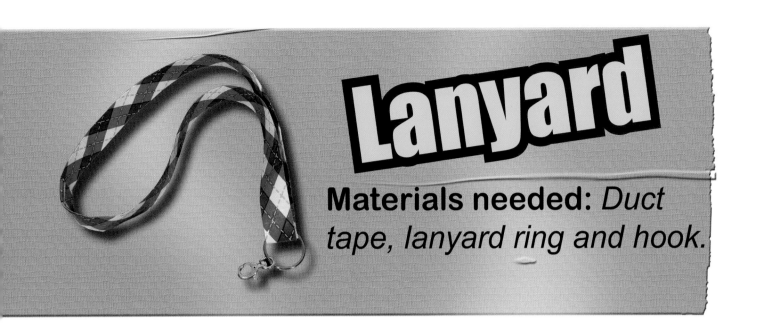

Lanyard

Materials needed: *Duct tape, lanyard ring and hook.*

Step one:

Cut two strips of tape approximately 18 inches long, depending on the length needed.

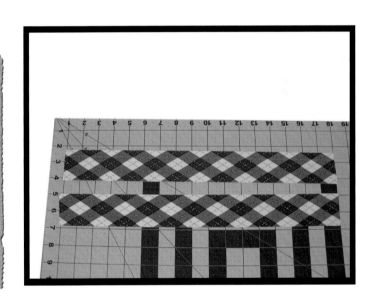

Step two:

Fold each strip in half, lengthwise. Use a middle to right, then middle to left motion to flatten the strips.

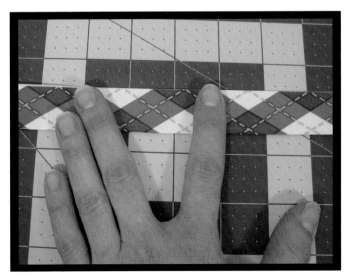

Step three:

Cut a 2 inch piece of tape and slice it in half, lengthwise.

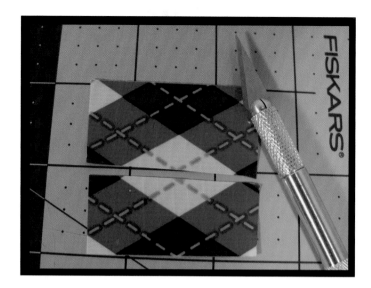

Step four:

Attach two free ends of your long straps by wrapping them with one of the 2 inch pieces.

Step five:

Fish the other loose ends through your lanyard ring, fold up onto the closest strap.

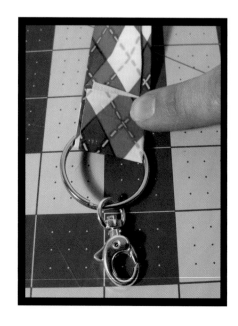

Step six:

Using the other 2 inch piece of tape, secure the folded edges to the top strap.

Step seven:

Hang IDs, passes, and keys off of your spiffy lanyard!

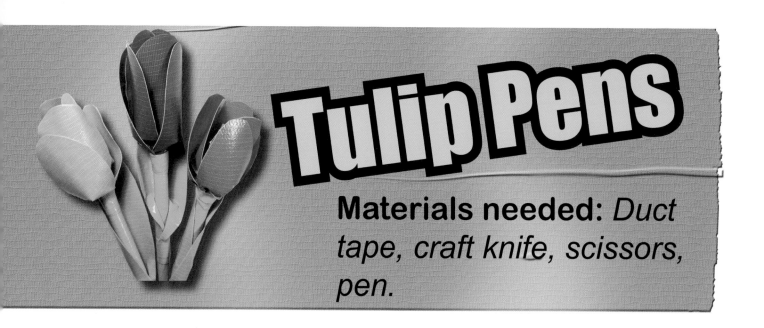

Tulip Pens

Materials needed: *Duct tape, craft knife, scissors, pen.*

Step one:

Cut a strip of green tape as long as a pen. Do not measure the tip area.

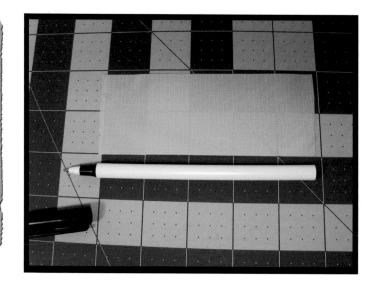

Step two:

Roll your pen into the tape evenly.

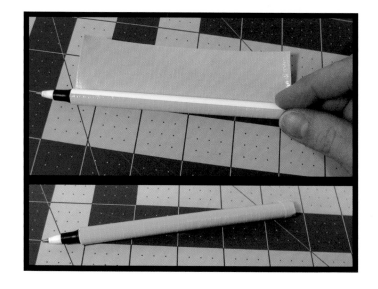

Step three:

To make the stamen, cut a 1 inch piece of yellow tape. Align it halfway off the end of the pen and wrap it all the way around.

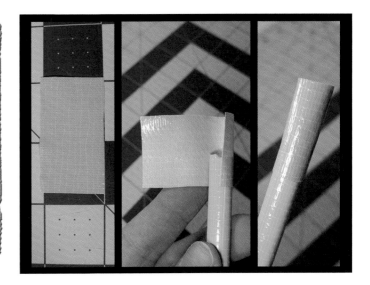

Step four:

Gently pinch the outer edges in toward the center, then gently pinch the other edges in.

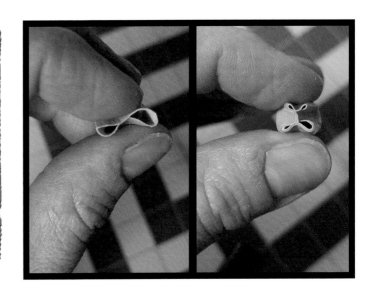

Step five:

Cut six 6 inch pieces of tape on your cutting mat.

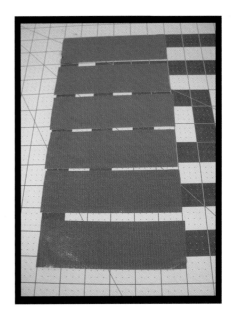

Step six:

Fold each piece in half, leaving 1/2 inch of sticky side exposed.

Step seven:

Cut a round petal shape out of each folded piece, using scissors. Use of a stencil is optional.

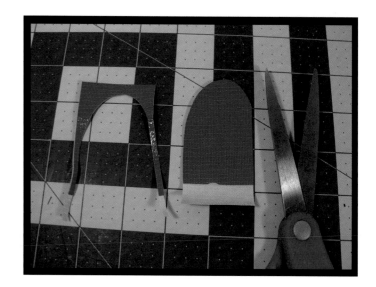

Step eight:

Cut a 1/2 inch slit in the center of each petal, on the bottom sticky side.

Step nine:

Overlap one half of the sticky edge onto the other to form a curved petal.

Step ten:

Wrap the petal around the pen so that all the sticky part is below the stamen.

Step eleven:

Repeat steps 7-10, wrapping the petals around the pen. Keep them as level as possible, offsetting each as you go.

Step twelve:

Cut one 10 inch strip of green tape and two 1/2 inch strips.

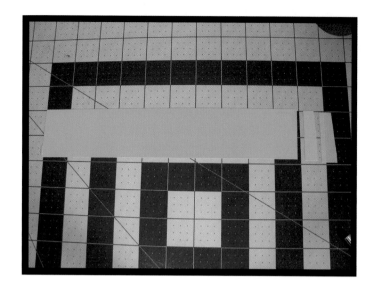

Step thirteen:

Wrap one 1/2 inch strip around the base of the flower to secure the petals.

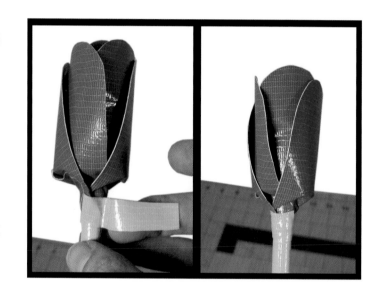

Step fourteen:

Fold the 10 inch strip over on itself, leaving 1/2 inch of sticky side exposed.

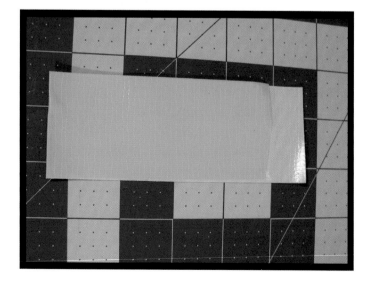

Step fifteen:

Cut a leaf shape out of the strip with scissors.
A stencil is optional.

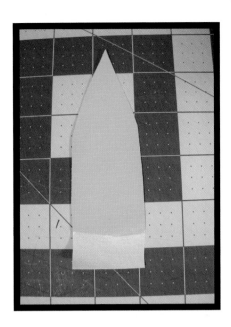

Step sixteen:

Wrap the leaf around the pen, about a quarter of the way up from the tip.

Step seventeen:

Use the other 1/2 inch strip to secure the leaf to the pen.

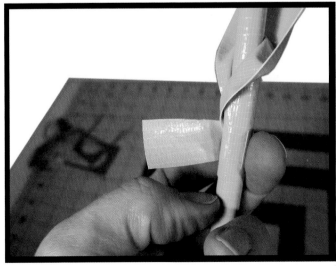

Step eighteen:

Fluff out the leaf and petals, and you are ready to write with style.

Pro Tips:

Use some of the other flower designs in this book to top your pen. A bouquet of flower pens in a can caddy (page 10) makes a great gift!

Blossoms

Materials needed: *Duct tape, scissors.*

Step one:

Cut a 6 inch piece of tape from your roll.

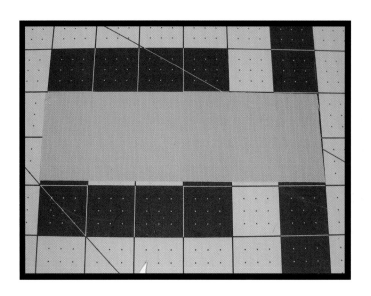

Step two:

Fold it 3/4 of the way back over on itself, lengthwise, leaving a quarter inch exposed.

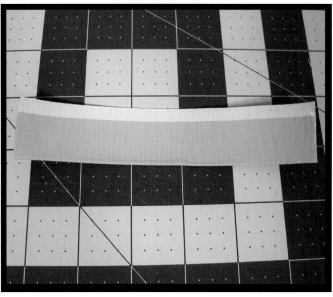

Step three:

Using scissors, make a small cut on every inch, close to the sticky strip, but not through it.

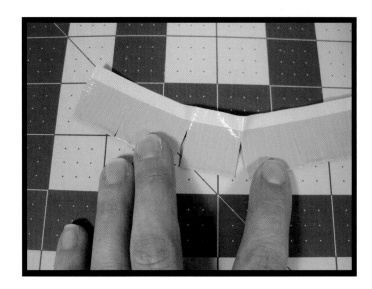

Step four:

Make an accordion fold with the first section by folding it in half, backwards, then re-folding the outer edges back to the center. Pinch the tape.

Step five:

Continue to accordion-fold each petal, pinching the sticky edge to secure. Close the end with tape or a dot of hot glue.

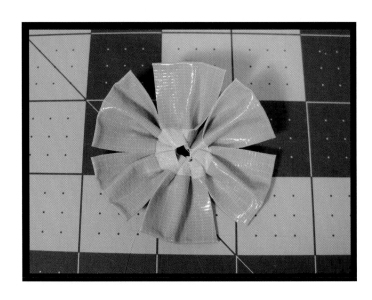

Step six:

Cut a 1 inch piece of tape for the center. Fold in half. Cut a circle out and shape it to fit the middle of your blossom.

Step seven:

Press the center onto the blossom, using the exposed stickiness to secure.

Step eight:

Using scissors, round out the petals.

Step nine:

Cut a 6 or 7 inch piece of tape for the stem.

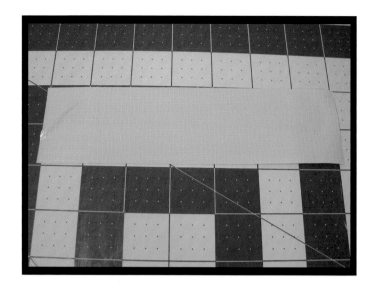

Step ten:

Using your finger to keep one side open, roll the tape tightly around itself.

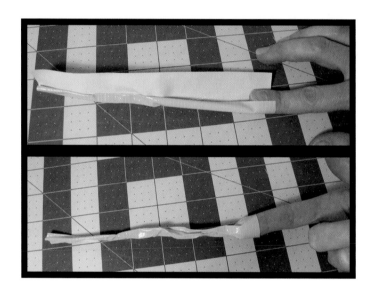

Step eleven:

Expose the open side by folding it out.

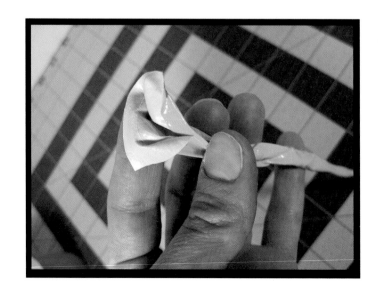

Step twelve:

Adhere the open end of the stem to the back of the blossom.

Step thirteen:

Make one or make a bouquet! Add a leaf, if desired, using the method on pages 42-43. Adjust the size of the leaf to your blossom.

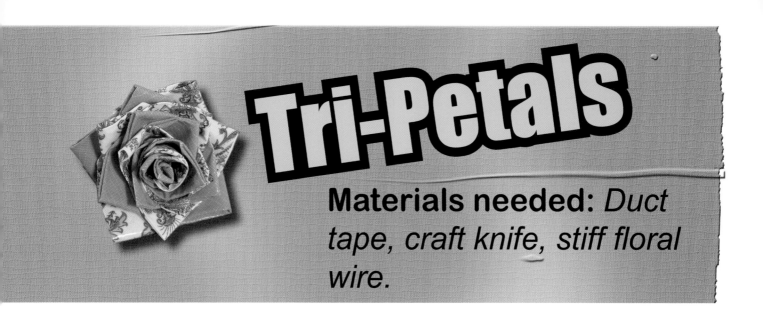

Tri-Petals

Materials needed: *Duct tape, craft knife, stiff floral wire.*

Step one:

Cut approximately 15-20 2 inch strips of tape.

Step two:

Fold the first corner over. The sticky side will make a "L" shape. Then, fold the other corner over to make a triangle with a sticky bottom edge.

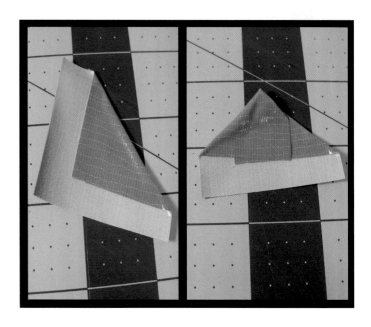

Step three:

Take a stiff wire and place the triangle on it. Wrap the tape tightly around the wire.

Step four:

Make your next triangle petal and wrap it around the first. Make sure to offset the next petal at an angle.

Step five:

Wrap the next triangle around the first two. Make sure each petal is offset and angled, so the petals will begin to open as you wrap them.

Step six:

Keep wrapping each triangle petal around the last and the flower will begin to fill out.

Step seven:

As the flower grows, there will be less wrapping and more placing of the petals. They should be slightly askew and overlap one another.

Step eight:

Once the desired fullness has been achieved, add the final petals.

Step nine:

To make the stem, cut a piece of green tape as long as your wire and roll the flower into it, wrapping it tightly.

Step ten:

Cut a 2 inch piece of green tape to match the stem.

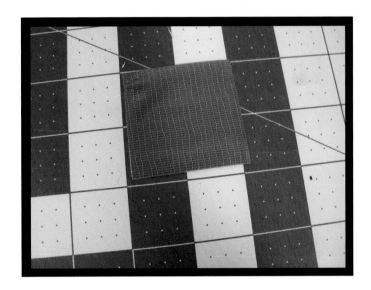

Step eleven:

Tilt the tape to make a diamond shape and attach it to the backside of the flower to secure the petals.

Step twelve:

Wrap the diamond piece around both the top of the wire and the bottom of the flower.

Step thirteen:

This piece will secure the lowest petals and bolster the stem.

Step fourteen:

Add a leaf, if desired, using the method on pages 42-43. Adjust the size of the leaf to your tri-petal flower.

Rose

Materials needed: *Duct tape, craft knife, scissors, stiff floral wire.*

Step one:

Cut a 4 inch piece of duct tape.

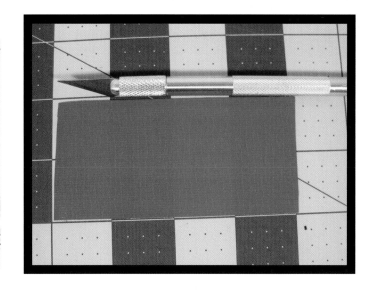

Step two:

Take a stiff wire and place it halfway up the sticky side of the tape.

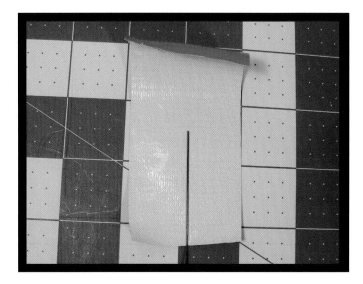

Step three:

Fold the tape over, leaving 1/4 inch of the sticky side exposed.

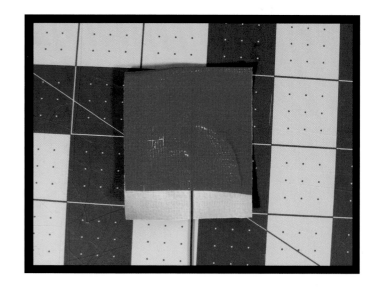

Step four:

Use scissors to round the petal.
Using a stencil is optional.

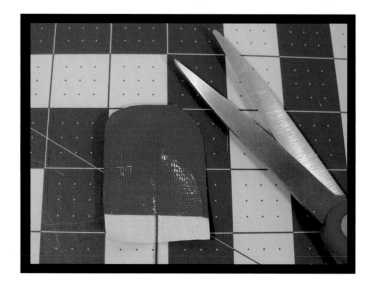

Step five:

Make 10-12 of these petals on stiff wire.

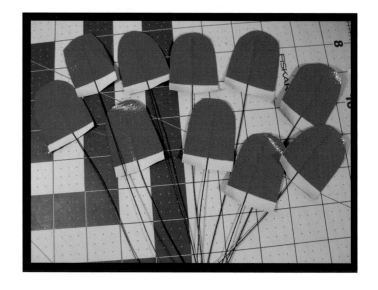

Step six:

Take the smallest petal and wrap it tightly around the wire.

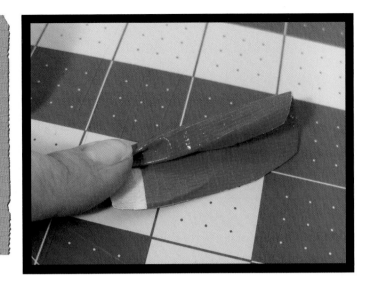

Step seven:

This will form the bud of the rose.

Step eight:

Take the next petal and wrap it around the first. Offset it slightly from the bud. Add a few pinched pleats in the sticky side as you wrap.

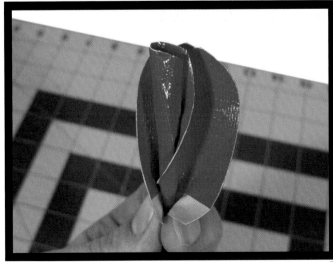

Step nine:

Push the top of the petal down, so the bottom bends outward, creating dimension.

Step ten:

Keep offsetting new petals around the last. Pleat the sticky part of the tape and push down on the petals for a realistic effect.

Step eleven:

Once the rose is full, open and "fluff" the petals to achieve the desired look.

Step twelve:

Twist the wires around each other, so they form one stem.

Step thirteen:

Cut a green piece of tape the length of the wires.

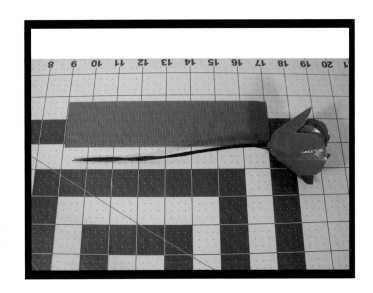

Step fourteen:

Wrap the tape tightly around the wires.

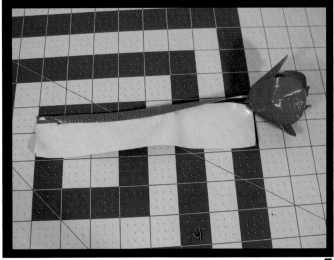

Step fifteen:

Cut two 3 inch pieces of green tape.

Step sixteen:

Fold them over, leaving 1/4 inch of sticky side exposed.

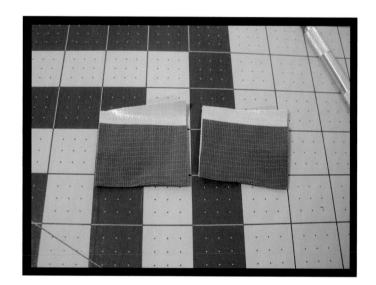

Step seventeen:

Using scissors, cut four slim triangles out. The sticky side should be at the base.

Step eighteen:

Wrap the base of the first triangle around the top of the stem.

Step nineteen:

Wrap the other triangles on each side.

Step twenty:

Add a leaf, if desired, using the method on pages 42-43. Adjust the size of the leaf to fit your rose.

61

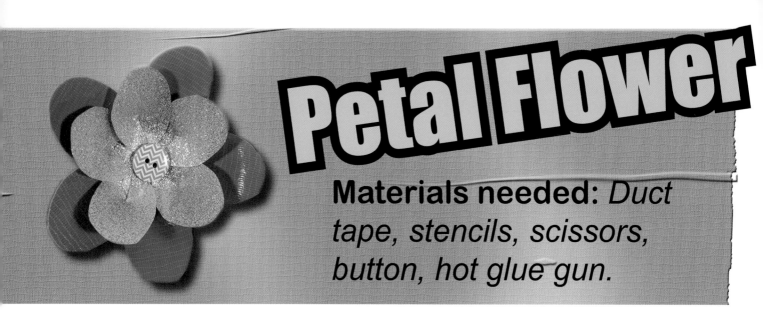

Petal Flower

Materials needed: *Duct tape, stencils, scissors, button, hot glue gun.*

Step one:

Create two oval stencils, one larger than the other. (See page 29, "How to Make Stickers")

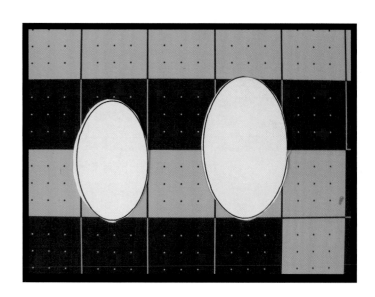

Step two:

Cut two pieces of tape the length of five petals for both sizes.

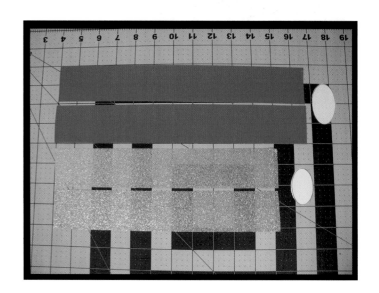

Step three:

Adhere the backs of each matching strip together. Trace five petals onto each strip and use scissors to cut out.

Step four:

Cut a 4 inch piece of tape and fold it in half. Use scissors to cut out a 1 1/2 inch to 2 inch circle. A stencil is optional.

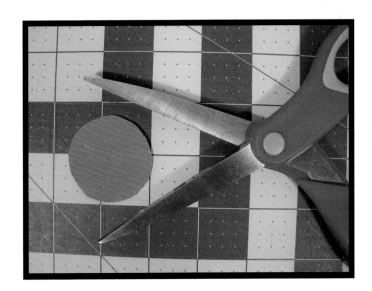

Step five:

Using scissors, make a small cut on the bottom of each large petal.

Step six:

Cross one side over the other to form a three dimensional petal and seal with a dot of glue.

Step seven:

Repeat steps five and six with the rest of the larger and smaller petals.

Step eight:

Glue the bottom of each large petal onto the outer half of the circle.
Fan them out evenly from the center.

Step nine:

Stagger the smaller petals in front of the larger ones. Seal with glue.

Step ten:

Glue a button, rhinestone or embellishment into the center.
Use hot glue or tape to apply the backing onto anything.

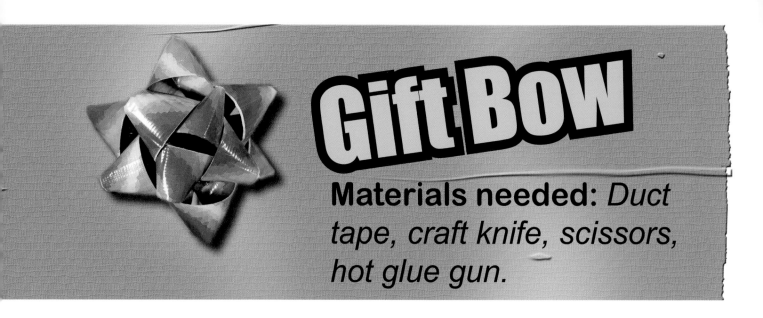

Gift Bow

Materials needed: *Duct tape, craft knife, scissors, hot glue gun.*

Step one:

Cut five pieces of tape from your roll. Measure about 9 inches long for a standard-sized bow.

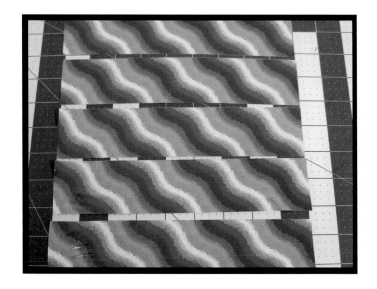

Step two:

Fold each piece in half, lengthwise.

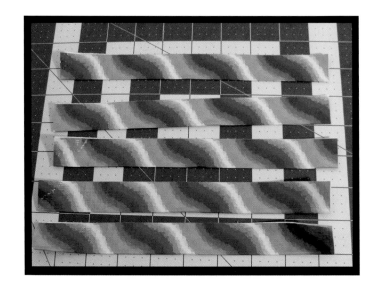

Step three:

Begin to form a "ribbon" shape, by folding the top half of a strip down and under the bottom half.

Step four:

Then fold it back up and around to make a figure eight, or infinity symbol.

Step five:

Secure with a dot of hot glue.
Make three of these as large as the ribbon will allow.

Step six:

Fan each ribbon on top of the next and secure with a dot of hot glue in between each layer.
Press to seal.

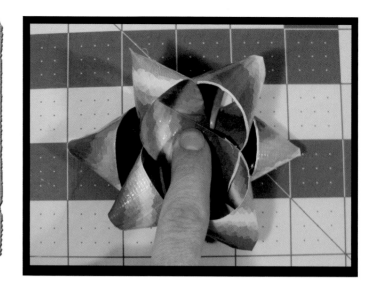

Step seven:

Using the larger ribbons as a guide, make a fourth, smaller ribbon that fits inside the first three. Trim any excess with scissors.

Step eight:

Secure it into the center with a dot of hot glue.

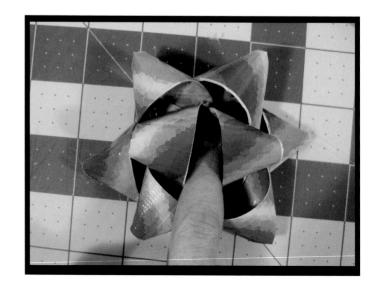

Step nine:

Using the fourth ribbon as a guide, make the fifth and smallest ribbon to fit inside the center.

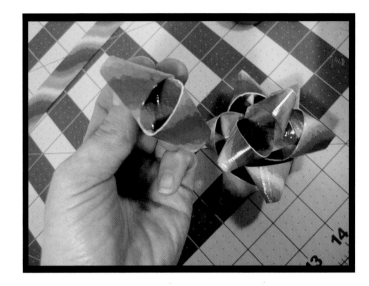

Step ten:

Press it into the center of the fourth ribbon with a dot of hot glue.

Step eleven:

Now you have a durable bow to decorate with or reuse again and again!

Chapter Three: Stuck on You

Enter the world of duct tape fashion and accessories.

Feather Earrings

Materials needed: *Duct tape, craft knife, stencils, earring hooks.*

Step one:

Create two feather stencils (see page 29). The larger one should be shorter than the distance from your ear to your neck/shoulder.

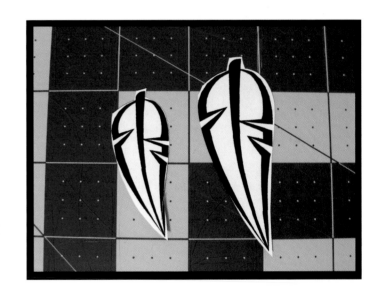

Step two:

Cut two pieces of tape slightly larger than your smaller feather.

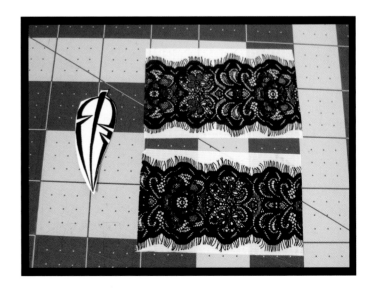

Step three:

Stick both pieces together, so each color or decorative side is facing out.

Step four:

Cut the shape out with your stencil, using your craft knife.

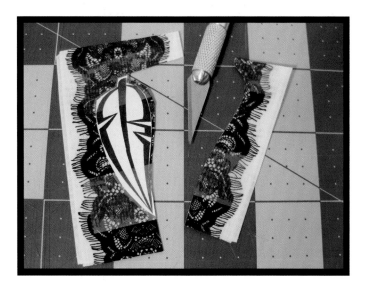

Step five:

Repeat steps 2-4 to create a match.

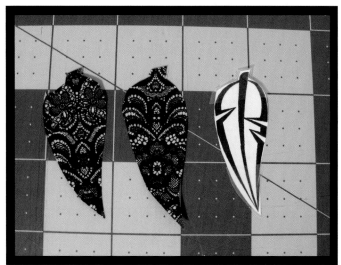

Step six:

Cut two pieces of tape slightly larger than your larger feather.

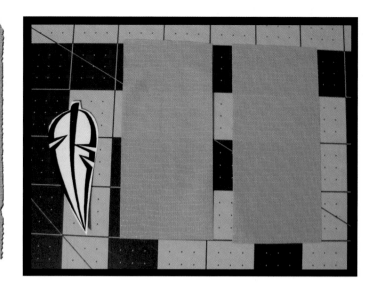

Step seven:

Stick the pieces together and cut the shape out with your craft knife.

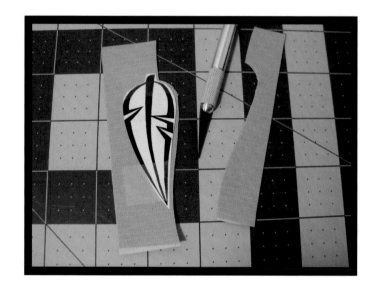

Step eight:

Repeat to make a match.

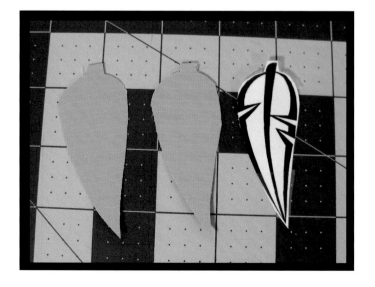

Step nine:

Using scissors, cut out small triangles to shape the feather.

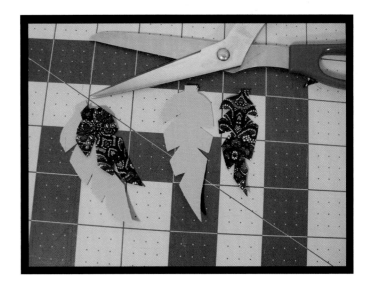

Step ten:

Place one of the smaller feathers on top of one of the larger feathers and make a small hole in the top for the earring clasp.

Step eleven:

Fish the earring clasp through the hole, making sure the hook is pointed back and away from the front of the design.

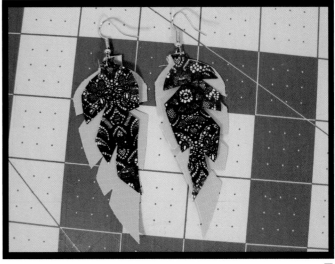

Bangle Earrings

Materials needed: *Duct tape, craft knife, stencils, earring hooks.*

Step one:

Create five cascading rectangular stencils between 3 inches, down to 1/2 inch (see page 29).

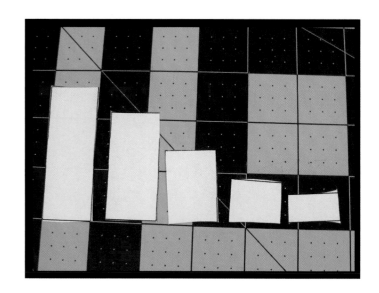

Step two:

Cut two pieces of tape larger than your largest rectangle.

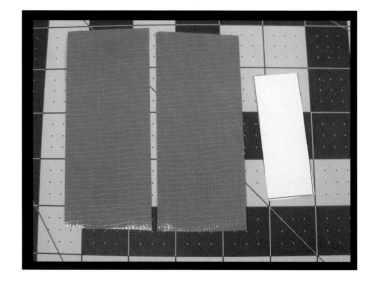

Step three:

Stick the pices together and cut the shape out with your craft knife or scissors.

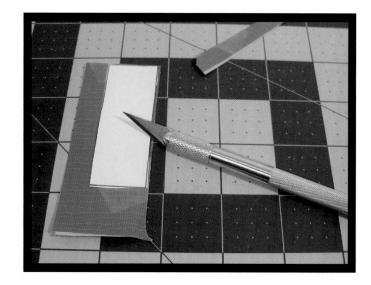

Step four:

Repeat steps two and three until you have two rectangles for each size.

Step five:

Cut the corners off each of the smallest rectangles to form triangles.

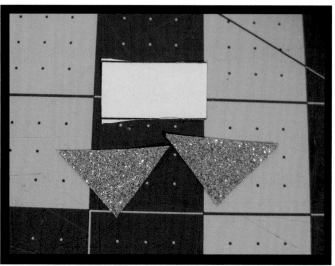

Step six:

Use the small triangles as stencils to cut the bottom corners off the next shortest pieces.

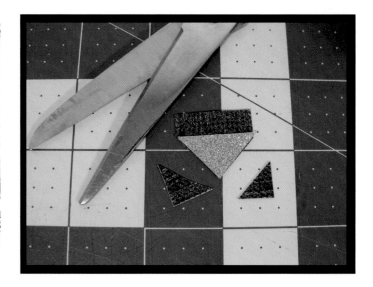

Step seven:

Continue to cut the corners off of all the rectangles.

Step eight:

Line up your cascading bangles in two rows.

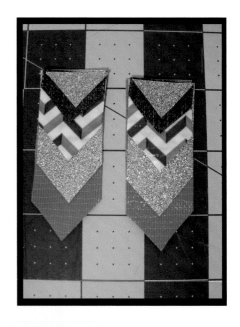

Step nine:

Once they are centered, poke a hole into the top, using a craft knife.

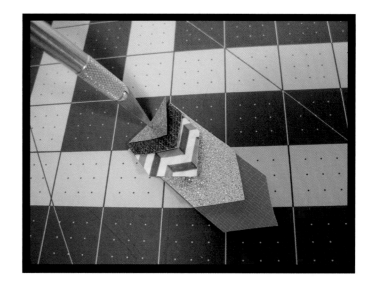

Step ten:

Fish the pieces onto your earring clasp. Make sure the hook is pointing back so the design will face outward.

Step eleven:

Use scissors to trim any unevenness and rock your chevron bangles!

Belt

Materials needed: *Duct tape, craft knife, belt loop rings.*

Step one:

Measure your waist and add 6 inches. Make a long, staggered, fabric strip (see page 105, "How to Make Fabric") with 10 inch segments of tape.

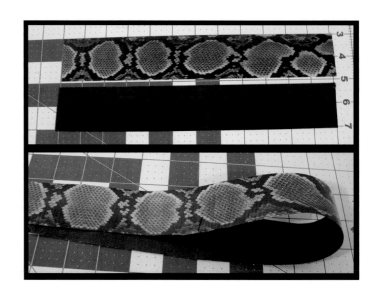

Step two:

Use a rubber-backed ruler and a craft knife to evenly trim the fabric to match the size of your belt rings.

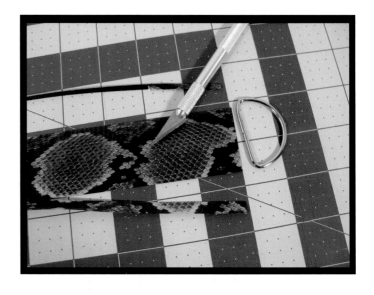

Step three:

Cut a 4 inch strip of tape. Fold the outside edge of your fabric over the belt rings, and onto the inside of your belt.

Step four:

Wrap the 4 inch strip around the edge to secure.

Step five:

Keep your pants up with style! Add an optional loop or embellishments for flair.

Woven Cuff

Materials needed: *Duct tape, craft knife, velcro tabs.*

Step one:

Measure your wrist and add 2 1/2 inches. Cut a piece of tape to match the measurement, then use a ruler and craft knife to slice 1/2 inch horizontal segments.

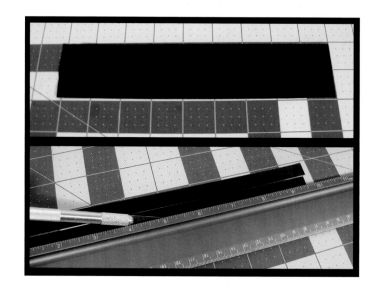

Step two:

Cut an equal piece of tape and slice it into 1/2 inch vertical segments.

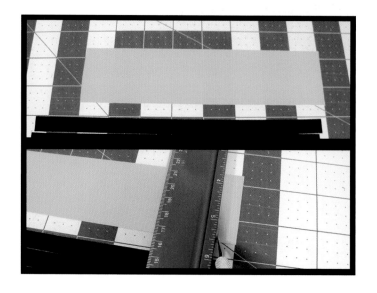

Step three:

Pull the first and third horizontal pieces back and lay a vertical strip down. Line it up with the bottom edge.

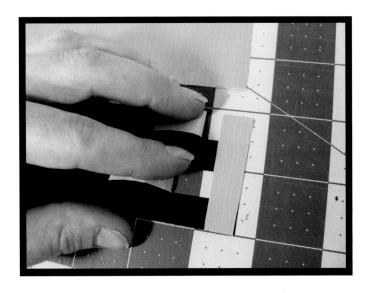

Step four:

Pull the second and fourth horizontal strips back from the opposite end. Lay a vertical strip down, lining it up with the top edge.

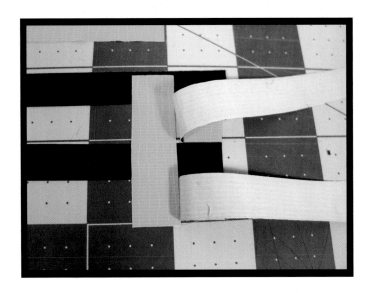

Step five:

Continue from the opposite side. Pull the first and third horizontal pieces back and lay a vertical strip down. Line it up with the bottom edge.

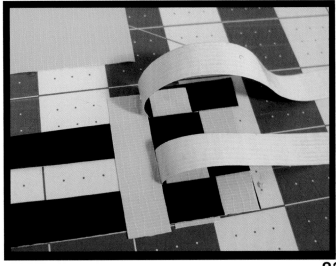

Step six:

Repeat steps 4-5, making a checkered pattern.

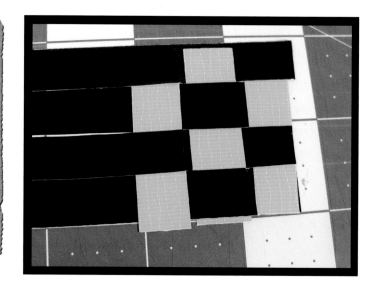

Step seven:

Once you finish, cut another piece of tape of equal length.

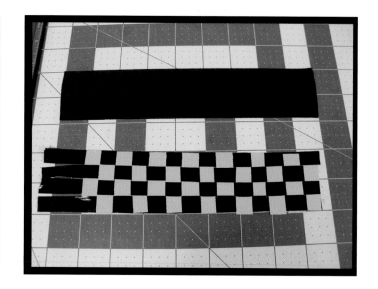

Step eight:

Adhere both sticky sides together.

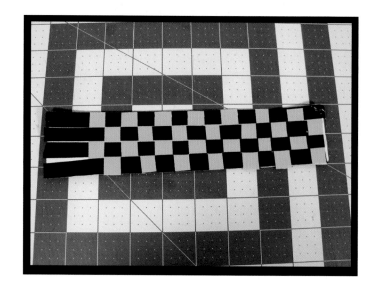

Step nine:

Cut two 1/4 inch or 1/2 inch strips of tape for the top and bottom borders.

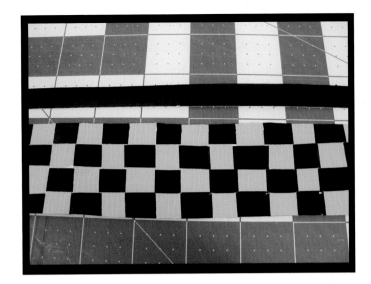

Step ten:

Line them across the top and bottom evenly. Fold them over the edges.

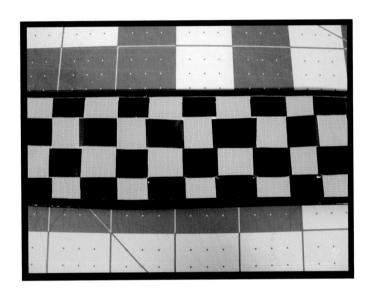

Step eleven:

Measure the cuff around your wrist again and trim off the excess.

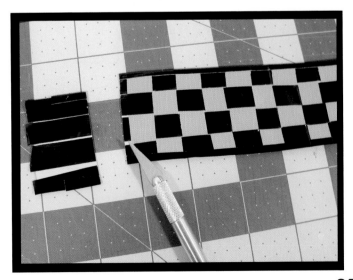

Step twelve:

Place velcro on the outside of one edge. Lay the other half of the velcro on top of it for even alignment.

Step thirteen:

Close the cuff around and press the velcro down to adhere.

Hair Bow

Materials needed: *Duct tape, scissors, barrette.*

Step one:

Cut one 8 inch strip of tape, one 6 inch strip of tape, and one 1/2 inch strip of tape.

Step two:

Fold the 8 inch and 6 inch pieces in half, then round the edges with a pair of scissors.

Step three:

Lay the smaller piece on top of the larger piece and pinch together in the middle.

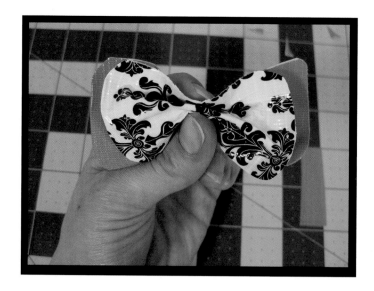

Step four:

Wrap the 1/2 inch piece of tape around the center to secure the pinch.

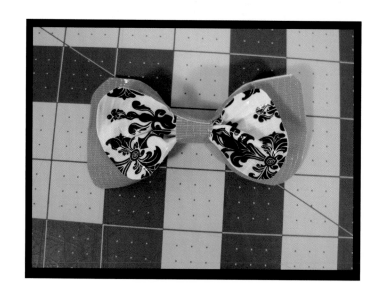

Step five:

Bend the smaller bow outward on each side to give the bow extra dimension.

Step six:

Cut another 1/2 inch strip and adhere it to the underside of the top of a barrette.

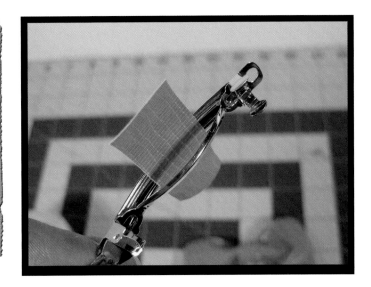

Step seven:

Wrap it around the center, on top of the first 1/2 inch strip.

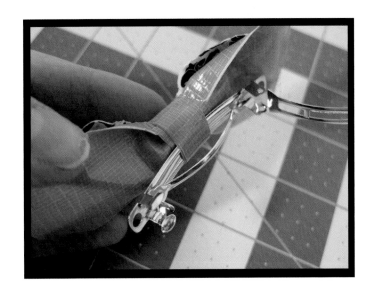

Step eight:

Doll up your hairdo or omit the barrette and glue the bow onto another project for a cute embellishment.

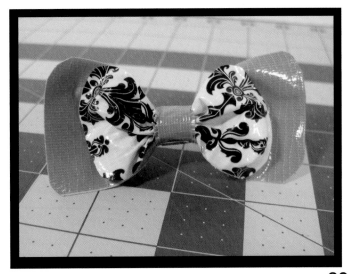

Wallet

Materials needed: *Duct tape, ruler, craft knife.*

Step one:

Make a fabric (see page 105, "How to Make Fabric") measuring 9 inches wide by 7 inches high.

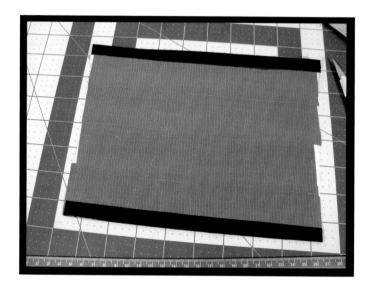

Step two:

Using a rubber-backed ruler and a craft knife, trim the uneven edges to measure 8 inches wide.

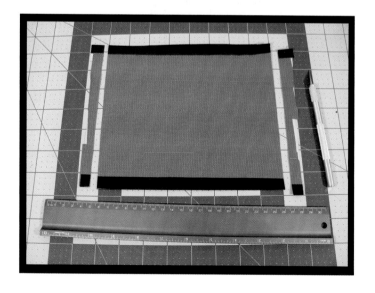

Step three:

Fold the wallet in half, lengthwise.

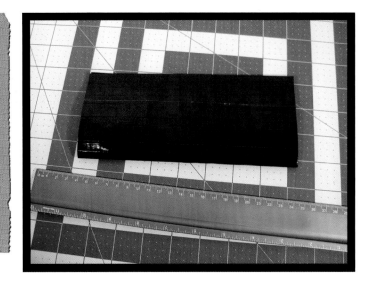

Step four:

Cut a piece of tape 3 1/2 inches long and seal the outer edges shut.

Step five:

This will form a long pocket for your bills.

Step six:

Fold your wallet in half.

Step seven:

Make three fabrics for pockets. Trim so that one measures 3 3/4 inches wide by 3 1/2 inches high and two measure 3 3/4 inches wide by 2 inches high.

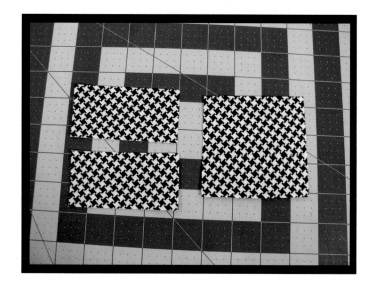

Step eight:

Roll out three 3/4 inches of tape.
Using a ruler and a craft knife, cut into 1/4 inch horizontal segments.

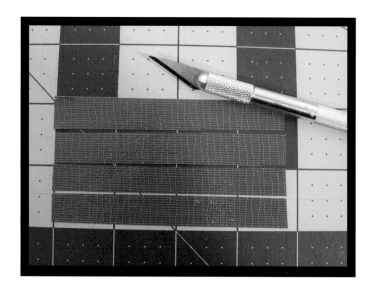

Step nine:

Fold two of the 1/4 inch strips over the top of the shorter fabrics.

Step ten:

Use the next strip to tape a short fabric into the side of the wallet, 1 inch up from the bottom.

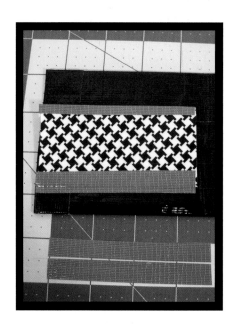

Step eleven:

Cut two 1/2 inch pieces of tape from your roll.

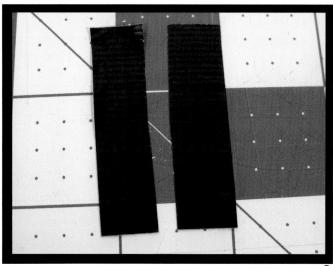

Step twelve:

Line the tape up exactly to the top of the pocket and tape the inside into the center.

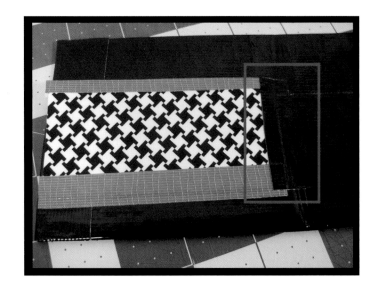

Step thirteen:

Line the tape up exactly to the top of the pocket and fold the tape over the front. Line the next pocket to the bottom of the wallet and tape the sides.

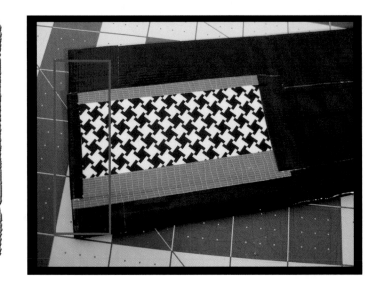

Step fourteen:

Take another 1/4 inch strip and fold over the left side edge of your larger fabric.

Step fifteen:

Cut a 3 1/2 inch strip of tape for the outer seal.

Step sixteen:

Affix it to the outer edge.

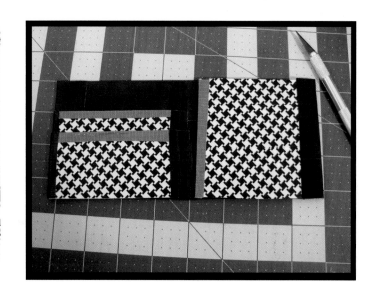

Step seventeen:

Cut a 3 3/4 inch piece of tape for the top seal.

Step eighteen:

Fold it into the top pocket of the wallet.

Step nineteen:

Cut an 8 inch piece of tape for the bottom seal.

Step twenty:

Fold it over the bottom edge to seal the pockets. Use your craft knife to make a small slit to open the bottom edge of the side pocket.

Step twenty-one:

There will be a large pocket for bills, a side pocket and two card pockets on the inside.

Step twenty-two:

Embellish the outside with stickers (see page 29, "How to Make Stickers") for extra style.

Tote Bag

Materials needed: *Duct tape, ruler, craft knife, four large brads or fasteners.*

Step one:

Make two fabrics 14 inches wide by 12 inches long. These will be the front and back of your bag.
(See page 105 "How to Make Fabric").

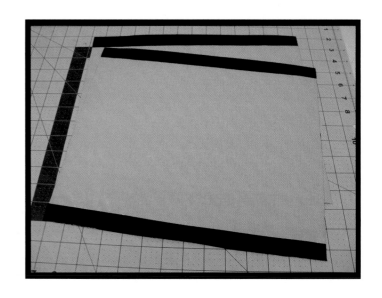

Step two:

Make two fabrics 12 inches high by 4 inches wide. These will become the sides of your bag.

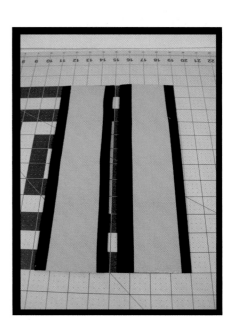

Step three:

Make one fabric 14 inches wide by 4 inches high. This will become the bottom of your bag.

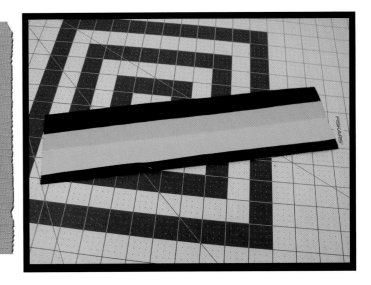

Step four:

Tape the sides of the bag to the back of the bag on the inside.

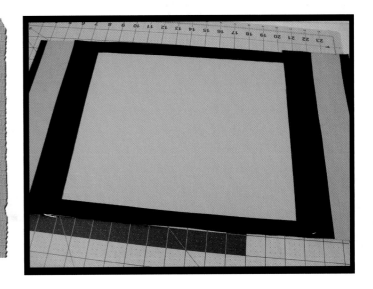

Step five:

Tape the sides of the bag to the back of the bag on the outside.

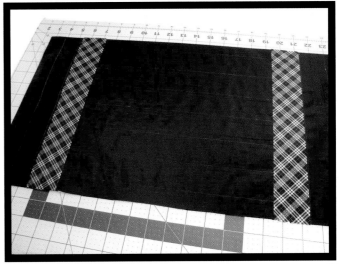

Step six:

Tape the bottom of the bag to the back of the bag on the inside. Trim any corner excess with a craft knife.

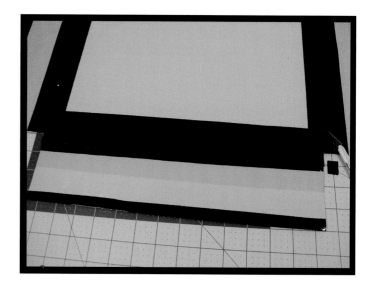

Step seven:

Tape the bottom of the bag to the back of the bag on the outside.

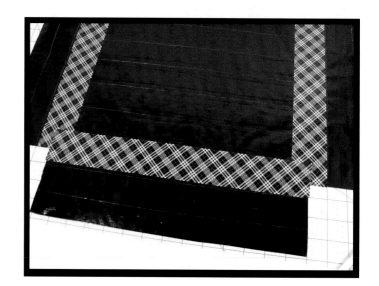

Step eight:

Tape the front of the bag to the bottom of the bag on the inside.

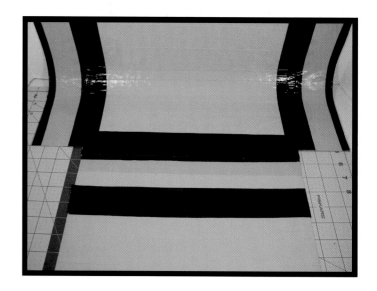

Step nine:

Tape the front of the bag to the bottom of the bag on the outside.

Step ten:

Fold the corners up, so the sides meet the bottom.

Step eleven:

Tape the corners and the open seams shut on the outside.

Step twelve:

Tape the seams shut on the inside of the bag.

Step thirteen:

To make an optional pocket, cut a fabric 14 inches wide by 6-8 inches high.

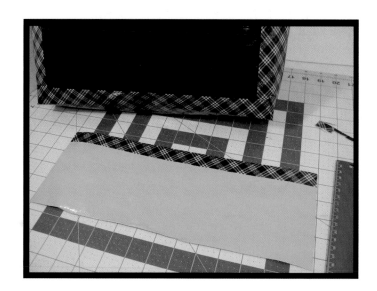

Step fourteen:

Tape the bottom inside edge of the pocket to the front of the bag.

Step fifteen:

Tape the outer edges of the pocket to the front of the bag on all sides and seal the bottom.

Step sixteen:

Make a strap by sticking two 24 inch strips of tape together.
(Repeat to make two.)

Step seventeen:

Round or angle the edges for a stylish effect.

Step eighteen:

Measure 4 inches from each end. Place the strap down 1 inch and make a small slit with your craft knife.

Step nineteen:

Apply a sturdy brad and tape the inside for reinforcement.
Repeat on all four sides.

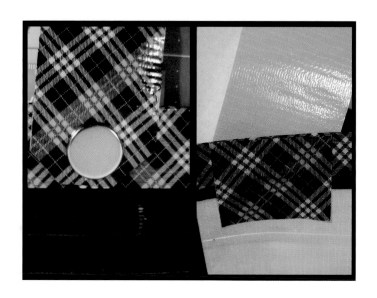

Step twenty:

Now you can tote just about anything - including all your rolls of duct tape!

How to Make Fabric

1.
Start by laying a strip of tape down on your mat, slightly longer than you need.

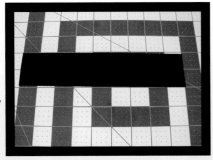

2.
Flip the first piece over, sticky side up, then lay out another piece of equal-length tape.

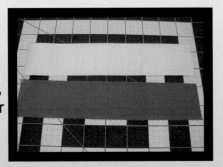

3.
Adhere the second piece to the back of the first, staggering a half-inch. Fold the bottom piece over the top edge.

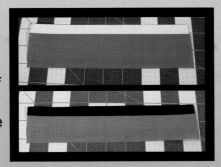

4.
Flip the joined pieces over and cut off another piece of equal-length tape.

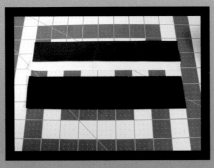

5.
Stick the new piece down, overlapping the first by 1/2 to 1 inch.

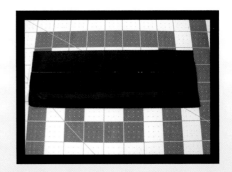

6.
Flip the joined pieces over and lay an overlapping piece on the other side.

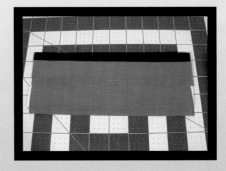

7.
Keep flipping the growing fabric over and adding to it until you reach your desired size. Fold the remaining overlap over the bottom edge.

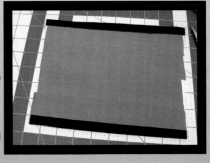

8.
Use your rubber-backed ruler and craft knife or scissors to trim the edges evenly to length.

Charms

Materials needed: *Duct tape, ruler, craft knife, hot glue gun, barrettes, clasps, hole punch.*

Step one:

To make a necklace, create a design of your choosing, stencils and embellishments are optional. Make sure your design is double-sided.

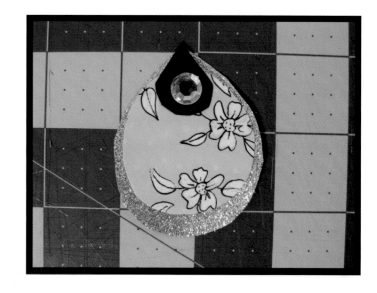

Step two:

Use a hole punch or a craft knife to poke a hole for a necklace clasp and apply.

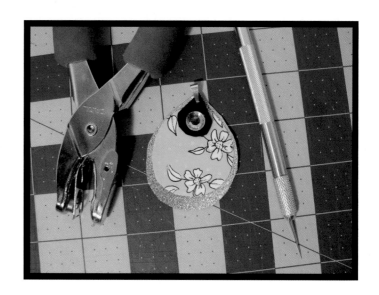

Step three:

Fish rope, line or a chain necklace through the clasp and you have a one-of-a-kind piece.

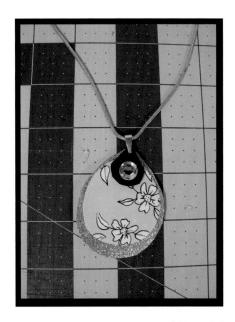

Step four:

To make a small barrette, create any flower design and a double-sided circle to act as a base.

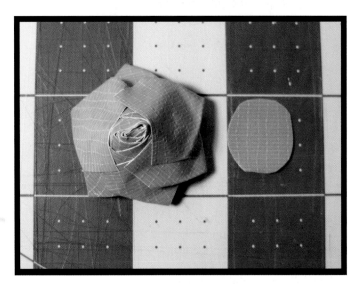

Step five:

Use a hot glue gun to adhere your flower to the circular base.

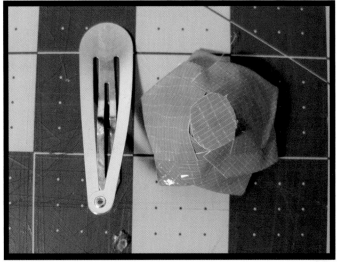

Step six:

Use a hot glue gun to adhere the circular base to the barrette. Allow it to completely dry before use.

Step seven:

If you have a larger design, use a larger barrette with a larger circular base.

Step eight:

Simply tape the clasp barrette to the circular base.

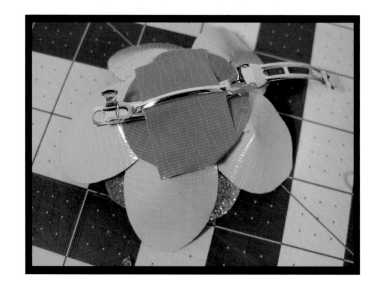

Step nine:

Another way to use a charm is to make a ring. Glue your circular base onto your flower and make a tight folded piece that matches the width of your finger.

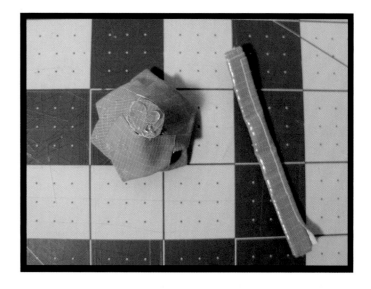

Step ten:

Turn the strip into a ring and adhere with a small piece of matching tape. Make sure there is room to slide it on and and off your finger.

Step eleven:

Use a hot glue gun to adhere your flower to the ring.

Stuck at Prom®

Get serious about duct tape fashion!

If you've done all the projects in this book and want to truly "tape" it to the next level, why not try designing your own prom attire? Duck® brand duct tape holds a yearly contest called Stuck at Prom® that puts your creativity and craftsmanship to the test! And the best part? You can win scholarship money for both you and your school.

The annual contest began in 2001, with the winners wearing duct tape attire in just two colors: yellow and black. It has since grown to showcase between 300-500 contestants a year, wearing amazingly elaborate color schemes and patterns. The attire is judged on workmanship, originality, use of color, accessories, and use of Duck® brand duct tape.

Since its inception, the contest has awarded hundreds of thousands of dollars in scholarships.

There are many different approaches to making a duct tape dress. Some fashionistas prefer using patterns and some like to use a dress form and see where their imagination takes them. Either way, it's best to start out with a design and color scheme before you start. It's also a good idea to have fabric on hand for your dress and suit lining for comfort and breathability. A simple internet search will put a world of ideas and tutorials at your fingertips.

Teens all over the country have made dresses, tuxedos and fabulous accessories to rock at prom. If you want to make a serious entrance that everyone will be talking about, strutting duct tape couture is a memorable way to go!

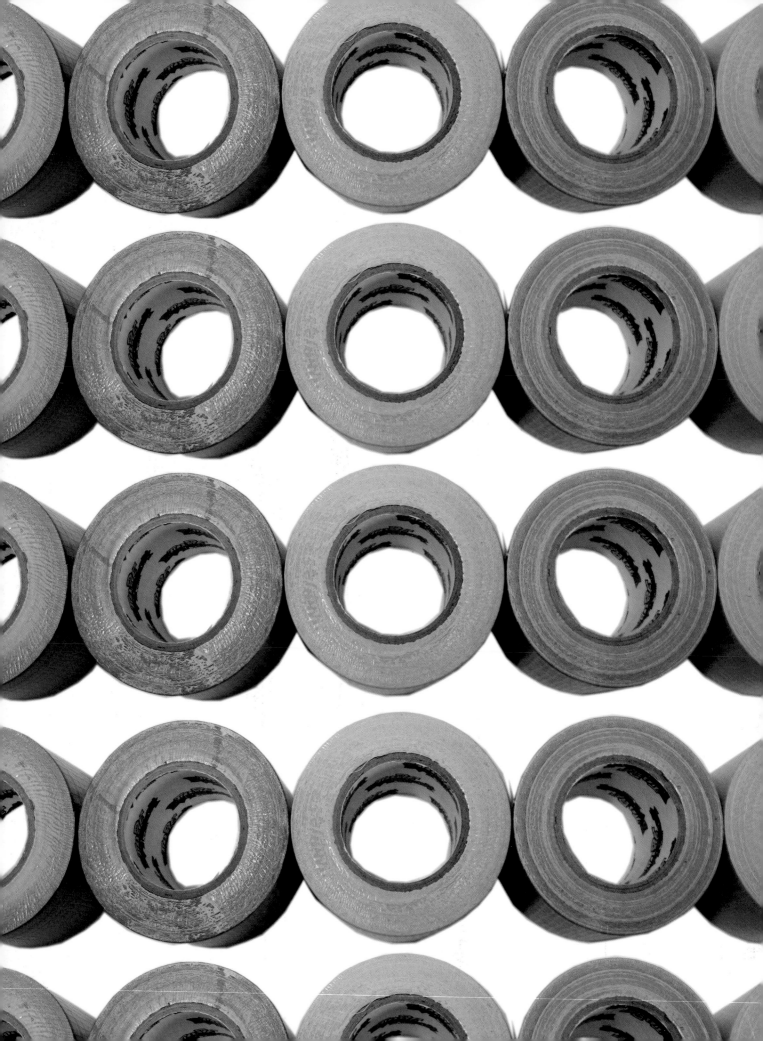